World Fusion Jazz: A Kaleidoscope of Cultural Confluence

By Abraham Ninan

An artistic illustration of World Fusion Music and Innovation

 WORLD FUSION JAZZ – Abraham Ninan

World Fusion Jazz: Painting the Universal Canvas of Sound

In the pulsating heart of jazz, where every note reverberates with the untamed spirit of artistic freedom, a mesmerizing realm unfurls its vibrant name - "World Fusion." In this enchanting domain, the boundaries of musical genres blur and dissolve, and the globe itself transforms into an infinite canvas of inspiration, painted with the hues of countless traditions. Within this captivating sonic landscape, three distinct subgenres emerge as luminous constellations amidst the night sky of creativity: Ethnic Fusion, Non-Western Fusion, and the frontier of Innovative New Music. It is within these celestial spheres that jazz intertwines seamlessly with the rich story of diverse cultural threads.

In the intricate mosaic of music, we see the reflection of life itself—a score inspired by the diverse threads of human experience. Every note, every rhythm, and every melody is a brushstroke on the canvas of our collective existence. World

Fusion Jazz embodies the very essence of this mosaic, where the boundaries between genres, cultures, and eras blur, revealing the interconnectedness of our global heritage. It is within this fusion, this alchemical transformation of musical elements, that we find the true magic of jazz. Jazz, at its core, is a universal language that transcends the limitations of words and communicates directly with the heart and soul. It is a language that knows no boundaries, a conversation that requires no translation, and an

An artistic illustration of Don Cherry

invitation to connect with one another on a profound and visceral level.

Exploring the Soulful Alchemy: Ethnic Fusion Jazz Unveiled

The artists we have encountered on our journey through World Fusion Jazz—Don Cherry, John McLaughlin, Don Ellis, Andy Narell, Django Reinhardt, and many more—are the pioneers who lit the torch of innovation. They blazed a trail into uncharted territories, and their music continues to inspire a new generation of torchbearers. These torchbearers, in turn, carry the flame forward, pushing the boundaries of what is possible and redefining the ever-evolving landscape of World Fusion Jazz. As we review this extraordinary realm, let us carry with us the unceasing spirit of exploration that defines World Fusion Jazz. It is a spirit that encourages us to celebrate the diversity of human expression, to embrace the beauty of cultural confluence, and to recognize that in the harmonious fusion of traditions, we discover the true essence of artistry. In this ongoing symphony of cultural confluence, we find the heartbeat of humanity, the rhythm of unity, and the melody of endless possibility.

In "World Fusion Jazz: A Kaleidoscope of Cultural Confluence," we celebrate the indomitable spirit of jazz, a spirit that continues to evolve, adapt, and inspire. It is a spirit that reminds us that, in the end, we are all part of the same beautiful composition—a composition, where the

An artistic illustration of a World Fusion Jazz Pioneer

music of the world unites us in a harmonious and timeless work of life.

In the throbbing core of jazz, where every note reverberates with the pulse of an untamed spirit, a mesmerizing realm unfurls its vibrant flag - "World Fusion." In this enchanting domain, the boundaries of musical genres blur and dissolve, and the globe itself transforms into a boundless canvas of inspiration, painted with the hues of countless traditions. Within this captivating sonic landscape, the three distinct subgenres emerge as luminous constellations amidst the night sky of creativity. It is within these celestial spheres that jazz intertwines seamlessly with the rich milieu of diverse cultural streams.

In the realm of Ethnic Fusion, the very essence of jazz harmoniously entwines with the myriad threads of cultural heritage. As the jazz idiom effortlessly melds with the traditions of various regions and peoples, a sonic alchemy of astonishing beauty ensues.

The listener is transported on a kaleidoscopic journey, where the hypnotic rhythms of Africa converse with the intricate melodies of India, where the soulful improvisations of American jazz intermingle with the haunting strains of the Middle East. In this fusion, borders vanish, and the human experience finds a universal voice, speaking through the eloquence of music.

Non-Western Fusion, another captivating facet of World Fusion,

An artistic illustration of John McLaughlin

compositions that challenge conventions and ignite the imagination.

The Innovative New Music Frontier, a beacon of boundless creativity, represents the cutting edge of World Fusion. Here, jazz pioneers push the boundaries of what is musically possible, blending genres in ways previously unimagined. It is a realm where experimentation reigns supreme, where electronic elements meld with acoustic instruments, where the past and the future collide in a dazzling display of innovation. Audiences are treated to a sonic odyssey that defies categorization, inviting them to embark on a thrilling voyage into unexplored musical dimensions. The readers are invited to embark on a literary and auditory adventure through these three captivating subgenres. Through vivid prose and insightful analysis, this book unveils the profound impact of World Fusion on the world of jazz and beyond. It celebrates the cultural exchange, artistic innovation, and spiritual resonance that define this mesmerizing realm. Prepare to be enchanted, enlightened, and enraptured as you delve into the heart of World Fusion, where jazz and culture harmonize in a symphony of boundless creativity.

Step into this enchanting world, where the boundaries of jazz dissolve like mist, and you will find yourself embarking on a journey through the mesmerizing ethnic melting pot of sound. Welcome to the realm of Ethnic Fusion Jazz, the first subgenre in our kaleidoscope of musical marvels. Here, the very essence of jazz

World Language of Jazz - An Artistic Illustration

 WORLD FUSION JAZZ – Abraham Ninan

between the soulful spontaneity of jazz improvisation and the enchanting melodies of diverse ethnic traditions.

In this captivating realm, one encounters the intoxicating rhythms of Latin jazz, a genre that pulses with the passionate heartbeat of the Americas. Within its vibrant core, the syncopated beats of African percussion, the romantic sway of Cuban melodies, and the fiery spirit of Spanish guitar all unite in a celebration of cultural convergence. It is a musical fiesta where structured compositions lay a sturdy foundation for the breathtaking jazz solos that effortlessly embellish them. Latin jazz is a testament to the power of fusion, where improvisation serves as the key, the alchemical ingredient that transforms familiar accompaniments and compositions into bewitching tapestries of sonic innovation.

Venture deeper into Ethnic Fusion Jazz, and you will discover the mystical allure of Indian music. Here, the ancient melodies of the East converge with the improvisational magic of jazz, forging a connection that transcends time and tradition. The intricate ragas and talas of classical Indian music find common ground with the expressive phrasing of jazz, creating a musical dialogue that resonates on a spiritual level. It is a journey of sonic meditation, where the notes themselves seem to breathe and pulse with life, inviting listeners to immerse themselves in a transcendent experience.

An artistic illustration of Django Reinhardt

WORLD FUSION JAZZ – Abraham Ninan

In Ethnic Fusion Jazz, improvisation is the secret alchemy that binds these diverse musical elements together. It is the spark of creativity that ignites in the hearts and minds of musicians, leading them to explore uncharted territory. Through improvisation, familiar compositions are reimagined, and accompaniments take on new life, becoming the canvas upon which artists paint their sonic masterpieces. It is a musical conversation where every note is a spoken word, every phrase a heartfelt response, and every performance a unique and ephemeral work of art.

As we delve deeper into the enchanting world of Ethnic Fusion Jazz, readers are invited to explore the rich history, cultural significance, and artistic brilliance of this subgenre. The story of Ethnic Fusion Jazz unfolds like a song itself, revealing the profound impact of this genre on the broader musical landscape. Join us on this musical odyssey, where improvisation and tradition collide, and where the boundaries of jazz are redefined in a song of sonic innovation and cultural harmony.

Sonic Horizons: Exploring Avant-Garde Jazz and Afrofuturism

As we continue our enchanting odyssey through the captivating world of World Fusion, the rhythms of Latin jazz linger in the air, their seductive allure beckoning us deeper into the heart of this musical fusion. Picture, if you will, a Latin jazz ensemble on a dimly stage,

An artistic illustration of Word Fusion music, if it had a face

their fingers caressing the strings of their instruments like a lover's tender touch. The pulse of congas and bongos sets the very heartbeat of the performance, while saxophones and trumpets weave intricate melodies through the velvety air. In this fusion, the syncopated rhythms of Cuba and the Caribbean meld effortlessly with the improvisational spirit of jazz, giving birth to an irresistible groove that moves both body and soul.

As the echoes of Latin jazz resonate in our hearts, we arrive at the second subgenre in our musical expedition: Non-Western Fusion. Here, jazz extends a graceful hand, inviting elements from specific non-Western musical traditions to join the dance. It is a harmonious partnership that transcends geographic boundaries, erasing the lines that separate cultures and histories.

Close your eyes, and you can almost feel the North African echoes infusing the jazz narrative in Dizzy Gillespie's haunting composition, "A Night in Tunisia." This iconic piece, a masterpiece in the annals of jazz history, is a testament to the genre's ability to absorb and reinterpret influences from far-flung corners of the globe. Gillespie's evocative trumpet melodies transport listeners to the ancient streets of Tunisia, where the mingling of North African and jazz motifs paints a vivid sonic landscape.

It is a musical conversation across continents, a dialogue between worlds, and a tribute to the enduring power of cultural exchange in music.

A Night in Tunisia - an artistic illustration

Non-Western Fusion, and you will encounter the innovative landscapes crafted by artists like Keith Jarrett. His quartet and quintet, recorded on the iconic Impulse label, embarked on an audacious expedition into the uncharted territory of Middle Eastern music.

Here, Middle Eastern instruments and harmonies are deftly reshaped into a mesmerizing soundscape that challenges the very definition of jazz. Jarrett's piano becomes a vessel for musical exploration,

Keith Jarrett - an artistic illustration

and listeners are invited to join in on this captivating journey, where the boundaries of tradition and innovation blur into a breathtaking horizon of sonic discovery.

You are now invited to experience the magical interplay between jazz and non-Western musical traditions. It is a story of musical diplomacy, where artists of diverse backgrounds converge in a harmonious dialogue, forging connections that transcend borders and

An illustration of lingering Latin Jazz music

WORLD FUSION JAZZ – Abraham Ninan

musical odyssey, where jazz extends its hand across continents, creating bridges of sound that enrich the Gaia of human expression. In Non-Western Fusion, every note is a passport to another culture, and every performance is a testament to the unifying power of music.

Exploring Cosmic Soundscapes and the New Music Frontier

As we survey the rich terrain of World Fusion, the echoes of Latin jazz and the enchanting melodies of North Africa still linger in our senses, guiding us deeper into the heart of this extraordinary fusion. Now, let us journey through time and space to explore the cosmic soundscapes of avant-garde jazz and Afrofuturism, a realm where pioneers like Sun Ra have left an indclible mark spanning from the 1950s to the 1990s.

Imagine a musical visionary like Sun Ra, whose artistic vision transcended conventional boundaries. His sonic discography is a testament to the boundless possibilities of jazz. In the hands of Sun Ra and his Arkestra, African rhythms gracefully intertwine with the jazz idiom, creating a cosmic journey where avant-garde jazz and Afrofuturism converge.

The result? A sonic landscape that defies earthly limitations, taking listeners on a transcendent voyage to the farthest reaches of the imagination. In this realm of limitless creativity, we also encounter the genius of extraordinary caliber.

An artistic illustration of Sun Ra and his Arkestra

Lateef, a musical alchemist of Lateef's contribution to the world of World Fusion is profound, as he fearlessly introduced traditional Middle Eastern instruments and methodologies into the jazz lexicon. Picture, if you will, the haunting, ethereal notes of the oboe merging seamlessly with the mesmerizing beauty of Middle Eastern scales. It is a fusion that transcends the mere boundaries of music. It is an invitation to explore the profound spiritual and cultural dimensions of sound.

Lateef's work, infused with a sense of reverence for cultural heritage and a thirst for musical exploration, opens a door to a world where diverse traditions harmonize. It is a place where the boundaries between East and West, ancient and modern, dissolve into a breathtaking mosaic of sonic innovation. Lateef's musical alchemy invites us to consider the deeper connections between music and spirituality, between the universal language of sound and the diverse universes of human belief.

You are now encouraged to embark on a cosmic odyssey through the avant-garde realms of jazz. It is a journey that pushes the boundaries of musical expression and challenges our understanding of the art form. Join us as we delve deeper into this extraordinary soundscape, where artists like Sun Ra and Yusef Lateef redefine the very essence of jazz, transcending earthly boundaries to create a music that resonates with the cosmic vibrations of the universe itself. In the world of World Fusion, the possibilities are as vast as the cosmos, and the music is an ever-

An illustration of Yusef Lateef and his album 'Eastern Sounds'

WORLD FUSION JAZZ – Abraham Ninan

expanding cosmos of creativity and innovation.

As we navigate the intricate labyrinth of World Fusion Jazz, our senses are heightened, and our journey takes us to the final subgenre, a realm where innovation knows no bounds. This is the New Music Frontier, a place where jazz improvisation entwines with the inventive aspects of existing ethnic traditions. Here, originality reigns supreme, yet the very essence of non-jazz traditions remains palpable. The result is

WORLD FUSION JAZZ – Abraham Ninan

An artistic illustration of Yusef Lateef

a harmonious blend that embodies the very spirit of cultural exploration.

The New Music Frontier: Exploring Genre-Bending Jazz Fusion with Don Cherry, John McLaughlin, and more

In this captivating realm of the New Music Frontier, visionary artists like Don Cherry and his ensembles Codona and Nu defy the confines of conventional jazz. They invite us on an extraordinary journey where the boundaries of jazz, world music, and avant-garde

Don Cherry and his Ensembles Codona and Nu - an illustration

experimentation blur into an indistinguishable mosaic. The borders between musical genres become permeable, and we find ourselves floating in a sonic dreamscape.

John McLaughlin, the virtuoso guitarist whose brilliance spans from the 1970s to the 1990s, stands as a testament to the transformative power of fusion. He boldly bridges the chasm between the intricate realms of Indian classical music and the improvisational prowess of jazz. His evocative compositions are a

Fusion Jazz Art

WORLD FUSION JAZZ – Abraham Ninan

harmonious interplay where the sitar's shimmering strings and the tabla's rhythmic dance seamlessly merge with the electric guitars and drum kits of jazz. It is a genre-defying symphony that resonates with the very soul of musical exploration. In the 1970s, the intrepid explorer Don Ellis ventured deep into uncharted territory, drawing inspiration from the mesmerizing music of India and the intricate rhythms of Bulgaria. Imagine the collision of Eastern scales and rhythms with the improvisational wizardry of jazz. It is a fusion that pushes the boundaries of what we thought possible in music, where each note is an exploration, each composition a journey into the unknown.

Fast-forward to the vibrant melodies of the 1990s, where Andy Narell mirrors the vivacious rhythms and instruments of Trinidad in his music. His compositions are a seamless interweaving of Caribbean culture, jazz improvisation, and funky grooves. It is a jubilant celebration of the Caribbean spirit, an invitation to move your feet and surrender to the infectious rhythms that evoke the essence of the islands.

We now embark on a final, exhilarating leg of our musical odyssey, one that transcends the limits of genre and tradition. The New Music Frontier is a testament to the ceaseless spirit of innovation that propels the world of jazz forward. It is a realm where the past and present coalesce, where the global realm of music is rewoven into a harmonious symphony of boundless creativity. Join us in this exploration, where the very

Cuban and Caribbean influence on World Fusion Jazz

essence of cultural fusion comes to life, and the frontiers of music are continually redrawn in the name of artistic discovery.

While our musical odyssey through the phantasmagoria of World Fusion Jazz has taken us on a mesmerizing journey across continents and decades, we must not forget that these remarkable fusions have deep and enduring roots that extend far beyond the realms of modern jazz. These musical tendrils of influence reach back through time, transcending geographical and temporal boundaries, connecting us to a rich milieu of cross-cultural collaboration. Even before the advent of what we now know as modern jazz, there were captivating glimpses of fusion that beckoned some of the earliest jazz musicians.

Bridging Cultures Through Time and Sound - From Polynesian Influences on the Mastery of Django Reinhardt

In our exploration of World Fusion Jazz, we find ourselves tracing these echoes to the early 20th century, where Polynesian

An artistic illustration of the Polynesian Music Scene

music had already embarked on its enchanting fusion with Western pop styles. This fusion, though not yet labeled as such, marked a pivotal moment in the evolution of music. It beckoned to some of the earliest jazz musicians, inviting them to partake in a cross-cultural dialogue that would lay the groundwork for the diverse fusion we witness today.

Picture, if you will, a time when the allure of Polynesian sounds began to captivate Western ears. The lilting melodies of ukuleles and the hypnotic rhythms of log drums wafted across the vast Pacific Ocean, casting a spell on those who encountered these exotic harmonies. Jazz musicians, ever the intrepid explorers of sound, could not resist the magnetic pull of these distant shores.

In the mid-20th century, this fascination with Polynesian music gave birth to the Exotica movement. Pioneered by artists like Martin Denny and Les Baxter, Exotica sought to recreate the sounds of far-off, tropical paradises within the

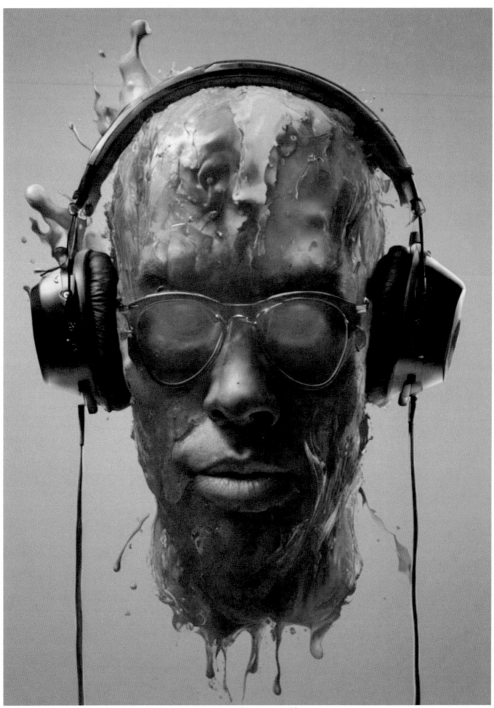

Martin Denny and The Exotic Sounds, an artistic illustration

WORLD FUSION JAZZ – Abraham Ninan

context of Western pop music. Utilizing a wide array of instruments and sound effects, they transported listeners to distant islands, sparking the imaginations of countless individuals and inspiring them to explore the world through music. This early exploration of Polynesian music, infused with the spirit of innovation and adventure, laid the foundation for the world fusion jazz we celebrate today. It serves as a reminder that the fusion of musical traditions transcends borders and defies time. It is a testament to the enduring human desire to connect, create, and explore the diverse nature of global culture through the universal language of music.

We now pay homage to these early pioneers who embarked on a musical voyage that would shape the very essence of jazz fusion. Join us as we continue to unravel the rich experience of world fusion jazz, where the past and present intertwine, creating a harmonious symphony that bridges the gaps between cultures and eras. It is a celebration of the boundless creativity of humanity and

Les Baxter - an artistic illustration

the power of music to unite us across time and space.

As we delve deeper into the fascinating narrative of World Fusion Jazz, we encounter an irresistible force that has coursed through the veins of American pop culture throughout the 20th century: the captivating allure of Caribbean dance rhythms. These rhythms, with their infectious energy and joyful spirit, have been a constant backdrop, an ever-present muse for improvisation, and a fertile ground for cultural melding by jazz artists. It is a reminder that fusion, in its many forms, has always been at the pulsating heart of jazz, even in its earliest manifestations.

In this vibrant setting of World Fusion Jazz, it is only fitting that we pause to pay homage to one of its true trailblazers: Django Reinhardt. In the smoky clubs of 1930s France, amid the heady atmosphere of artistic innovation, Reinhardt embarked on a remarkable and transcendent journey. Armed with his virtuoso guitar skills, he seamlessly

Revisiting Django again!

merged the traditions of Gypsy music with the elegance of French impressionist concert music and the unfettered improvisational spirit of jazz.

Picture, if you will, the magical alchemy that took place as Reinhardt's fingers danced across the frets of his guitar. The fiery passion of Gypsy music entwined with the intricate beauty of French impressionism. All the while it is infused with the electrifying spontaneity of jazz. It was a fusion of worlds, a convergence of cultural landscapes that defied easy categorization. Django Reinhardt's music, characterized by its dazzling virtuosity and heartfelt emotion, remains a testament to the enduring power of cultural confluence.

Reinhardt's legacy echoes resoundingly through the annals of jazz history. His music, like a beautifully constructed bridge, connects the worlds of Europe and America, Gypsy and jazz, tradition, and innovation. It serves as a lasting inspiration for generations of musicians who follow in his footsteps, a reminder that music is a language that transcends borders and a testament to the transformative nature of fusion.

In "World Fusion Jazz: A Kaleidoscope of Cultural Confluence," we honor Django Reinhardt as a pioneer whose artistic journey exemplifies the essence of world fusion jazz. His music serves as a bridge, spanning cultures and eras, and reminds us that the most captivating moments in jazz history are often born from the fusion of diverse musical traditions.

European influences - World Fusion Jazz.

 WORLD FUSION JAZZ – Abraham Ninan

Join us as we continue to explore this traditions and the jubilant celebration of the human spirit's insatiable thirst for exploration. It is here that we find a testament to the boundless power of the universal language of music—a language that effortlessly transcends borders, defies categorization, and unites disparate traditions.

It is an invitation to partake in a symphony, a harmonious symphony, where the world's cultures, rhythms, and melodies converge in a dazzling display of creative brilliance. The essence of fusion, as we have discovered throughout our musical odyssey, is not merely a merging of notes or styles.

It is a profound and enduring journey that mirrors the human experience itself—a journey that transcends time, place, and circumstance. It is the shared longing for connection, the irresistible urge to communicate, and the timeless impulse to create. In this magnificent journey, we bear witness to

An artistic impression of a Jazz Saxophonist

the resilience of the human spirit, which, like the music itself, is boundless in its capacity to evolve, adapt, and inspire.

Bridging Cultures, Inspiring Unity, and Celebrating Boundless Creativity

The artists we have encountered on this voyage—Don Cherry, John McLaughlin, Don Ellis, Andy Narell, Django Reinhardt, and countless others—are not merely musicians. They are messengers. They carry with them the stories of cultures, the echoes of distant lands, and the dreams of generations. Through their music, they build bridges across chasms of misunderstanding, welcoming us into the rich backdrop of the world's cultural heritage.

In this book, we celebrate this unity of cultures, where jazz becomes the common tongue spoken by people of diverse backgrounds and experiences. It is a reminder that at our core, we are all connected by the shared human experience, and music serves as a

An artistic illustration of Gypsy Jazz.

WORLD FUSION JAZZ – Abraham Ninan

powerful catalyst for understanding and empathy. Through world fusion jazz, we are given the chance to embark on a profound and soul-enriching journey— one that opens our hearts to the beauty of diversity, the richness of tradition, and the boundless possibilities of artistic expression.

As we conclude our exploration of this captivating realm, let us carry with us the spirit of world fusion jazz—the spirit of cultural confluence, collaboration, and creativity. It is a force that reminds us that in the face of division, music can be a unifying force. In the depths of complexity, simplicity can be found in a single note. And in the grand map of our world, we are all fragments held together in a harmonious cartography of humanity.

As we stand on the precipice of the vast expanse that is World Fusion Jazz, we are reminded that the spirit of exploration within this genre remains unceasing. It is a beckoning call, a siren song that urges us to venture beyond the boundaries of

An artistic impression of a World Fusion Jazz artist

WORLD FUSION JAZZ – Abraham Ninan

the familiar, to embrace the unknown, and to uncover the endless possibilities that emerge when cultures collide in harmonious dialogue. It is, in essence, a profound invitation to journey—an invitation to embark on a musical odyssey where creativity knows no limits, and the horizon is ever-expanding.

In the intricate mosaic of music, we see the reflection of life itself—one that is comprised of variegated instances of human experience. Every note, every rhythm, and every melody is a brushstroke on the canvas of our collective existence. World Fusion Jazz embodies the very essence of this mosaic, where the boundaries between genres, cultures, and eras blur, revealing the interconnectedness of our global heritage.

It is within this fusion, this alchemical transformation of musical elements, that we find the true magic of jazz. Jazz, at its core, is a universal language that transcends the limitations of words and

Harmonious Cool Jazz - an artistic illustration

communicates directly with the heart and soul. It is a language that knows no boundaries, a conversation that requires no translation, and an invitation to connect with one another on a profound and visceral level.

The artists we have encountered on our journey through World Fusion Jazz— Don Cherry, John McLaughlin, Don Ellis, Andy Narell, Django Reinhardt, and many more—are the pioneers who lit the torch of innovation. They blazed a trail into uncharted territories, and their music continues to inspire a new generation of torchbearers. These torchbearers, in turn, carry the flame forward, pushing the boundaries of what is possible and redefining the ever-evolving landscape of World Fusion Jazz.

Let us carry with us the unceasing spirit of exploration that defines World Fusion Jazz. It is a spirit that encourages us to celebrate the diversity of human expression, to embrace the beauty of cultural confluence, and to recognize that in the harmonious fusion of traditions,

World Fusion Jazz Saxophonist Duo

we discover the true essence of artistry. In this ongoing symphony of cultural confluence, we find the heartbeat of humanity, the rhythm of unity, and the melody of endless possibility. We thus celebrate the indomitable spirit of jazz, a spirit that continues to evolve, adapt, and inspire. It is a spirit that reminds us that, in the end, we are all part of the same beautiful composition—a composition where the music of the world unites us in a harmonious and timeless symphony of life.

Harmonizing the Cosmos: The Grand Finale of World Fusion Jazz

In the grand finale of our journey through the kaleidoscope of World Fusion Jazz, we find ourselves at the crossroads of culture and creativity, where the boundaries of tradition and innovation cease to exist.

Here, in this mesmerizing realm, jazz transcends its earthly constraints and soars into the infinite cosmos of possibility.

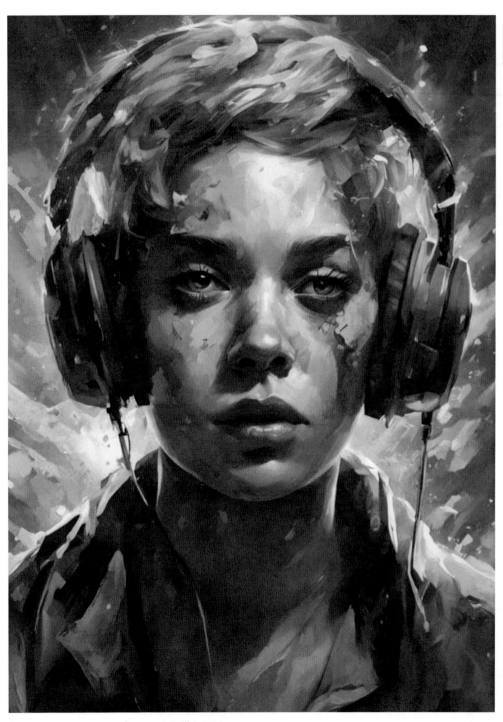

Innovative new music enjoyed - an artistic illustration

 WORLD FUSION JAZZ – Abraham Ninan

It is a culmination of human ingenuity, a testament to the universal language of music, and a celebration of the boundless power of cultural confluence. In the heart of World Fusion Jazz, we discover a profound truth: that music, like the human spirit itself, is a force of nature, constantly evolving, adapting, and expanding.

It reflects our collective history, a mirror of our shared experiences, and a testament to our ceaseless quest for connection and expression.

The artists we have encountered on this epic voyage—Don Cherry, John McLaughlin, Don Ellis, Andy Narell, Django Reinhardt, and countless others—are the cosmic navigators of sound, charting unexplored constellations of musical possibility.

They remind us that the boundaries of creativity are limited only by our willingness to explore, to collaborate, and to be inspired by the rich tapestry of global culture.

World Fusion Jazz Aficionado

WORLD FUSION JAZZ – Abraham Ninan

As we bid farewell to the enchanting world of World Fusion Jazz, let us carry with us the spirit of exploration, the harmony of diversity, and the symphony of unity.

It is a spirit that transcends time and space, a melody that resonates with the essence of our shared humanity, and a call to continue our never-ending quest for musical enlightenment.

In the end, World Fusion Jazz is more than a genre. It is a testament to the enduring power of human creativity, the unifying force of music, and the limitless possibilities of artistic expression. It continues to echo through the ages, connecting us all in the universal language of jazz.

Made in the USA
Monee, IL
21 June 2024

4928016a-662d-45c7-a782-3907610e1214R02